MS Outlook

Davinder Singh Minhas

RISING SUN

RISING SUN

RISING SUN

an imprint of
New Dawn Press

NEW DAWN PRESS GROUP

New Dawn Press, Inc., 244 South Randall Rd # 90, Elgin, IL 60123

e-mail: sales@newdawnpress.com

New Dawn Press, 2 Tintern Close, Slough, Berkshire, SL1-2TB, UK

e-mail: ndpuk@newdawnpress.com
        sterlingdis@yahoo.co.uk

New Dawn Press (An Imprint of Sterling Publishers (P) Ltd.)

A-59, Okhla Industrial Area, Phase-II, New Delhi-110020

e-mail: sterlingpublishers@touchtelindia.net
        Ghai@nde.vsnl.net.in

© 2005, New Dawn Press

Printed at Sterling Publishers (P) Ltd., New Delhi-110020.

Contents

1. Introduction   5

2. Checking Mails   14

3. Calender   18

4. Using Tasks   27

5. Contacts   32

1. Introduction

Microsoft Outlook is an application of Microsoft Office. This is a powerful tool of **Personal Information Management (PIM)** program that helps a person in organizing his schedule, keep track of one's contacts and communicate with others. Generally, people have several appointments to keep and tasks to accomplish in a day, week, or month. Outlook helps by maintaining schedule and by organizing the information in a structured and readable manner. By having this facility, one can keep a track of meetings, e-mail messages, and notes with a particular contact. This organization consists of Outlook's Calendar, Contacts, Tasks, and Notes. Contact information can be found via Find option, which can be accessed from the calendar, e-mail, and other Outlook components. PIMs give an opportunity to individuals and workgroups to organize, find, view, and share information in the most convenient way.

Starting Outlook

To start Outlook, Windows must be running. Perform the following steps to start Outlook:

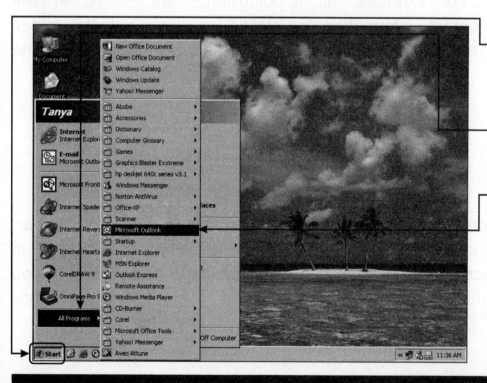

1. Click on the **start** button. The start menu will appear.

2. Click on **All Programs**.

3. In the All Programs submenu, click on **Microsoft Outlook**.

*The **Microsoft Outlook** window appears after a few moments.*

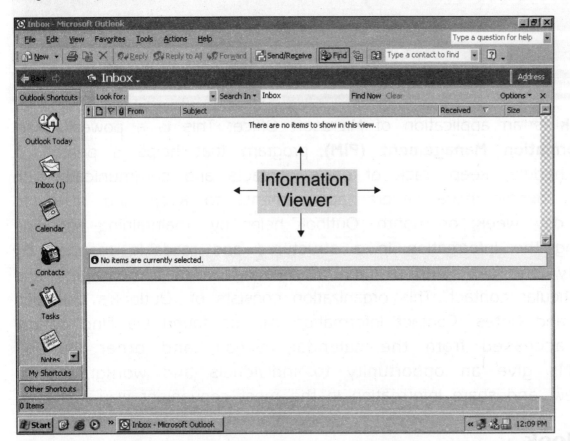

Outlook displays the Inbox folder in the Inbox - Microsoft Outlook window.

Outlook is organized around groups of **items,** such as Outlook Today, Inbox, Calendar, Contacts, Tasks, and Notes. Groups of the same type are stored in the same Outlook folder. For example, all appointments are stored in the Calendar folder, and all contact information is stored in the Contacts folder. When a folder is opened, the items in the selected folder get displayed in the **Information Viewer**.

Using Outlook Bar

On the left side of the screen, there is a gray column called the **Outlook bar.** The Outlook bar contains icons that allow you to change what is displayed in the information viewer. Each icon represents a shortcut to a folder. When you first start Outlook, the information viewer displays the contents of the Inbox folder.

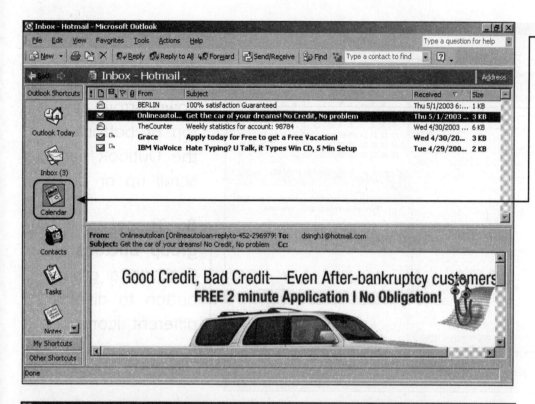

1. Click on any **Icon**. In this example, we choose the Calender.

The items associated with the icon will appear in the information viewer, which is shown in the next screen.

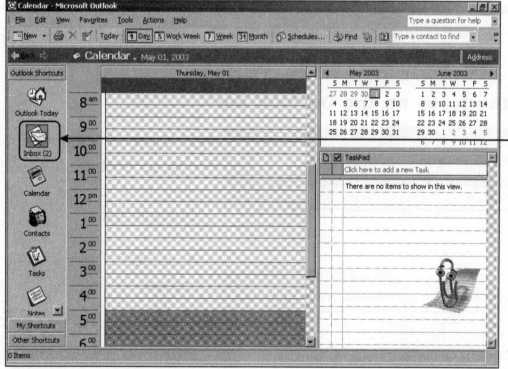

2. Click on the **Inbox** icon.

E-mail messages will appear again once this icon is clicked.

There are many icons on the Outlook bar that are not immediately visible on the screen. The **Scroll bar** arrows can be clicked to see more icons, or switch on to a different Outlook group. The default Outlook groups are Outlook Shortcuts, My Shortcuts, and Other Shortcuts.

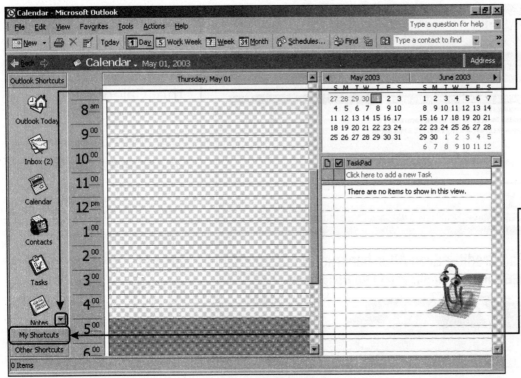

A. These are **scroll bar arrows**. Click on the up or down arrow at the top or bottom of the Outlook bar to scroll up or down.

B. These are **group buttons.** Click on a group button to display different icons.

An Outlook group is a way to organize folders on the Outlook bar. By clicking on the right mouse button on the Outlook bar, you can add, delete, or rename the Outlook groups.

Change the Size of the Icons on the Outlook Bar

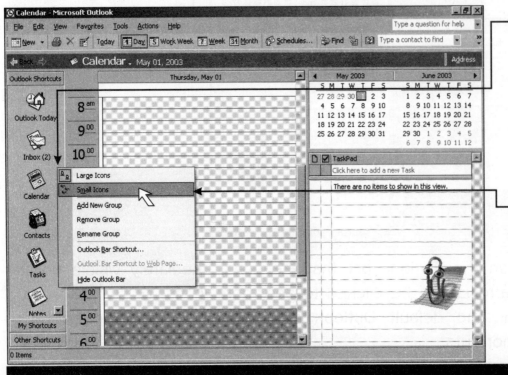

1. Click on the right mouse button in a gray area of the Outlook bar.

A shortcut menu will appear.

2. Click on an **icon size** with the mouse button. The size of the icons will get increased or reduced accordingly.

Folder List

You can use the folder list to navigate in Outlook. The icons are also known as Folders that appear on the Outlook bar.

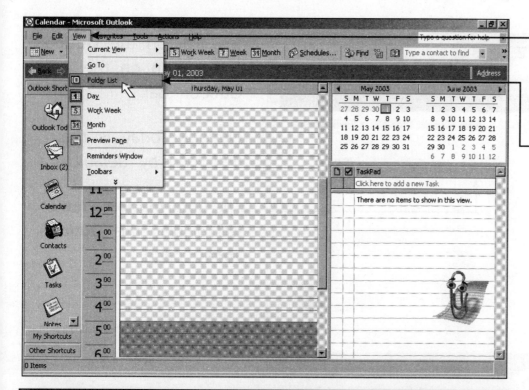

1. Click on **View.**

*The **View** menu will appear.*

2. Click on the **Folder List.**

*A **pane** will open next to the Outlook bar that will allow you to navigate your folders.*

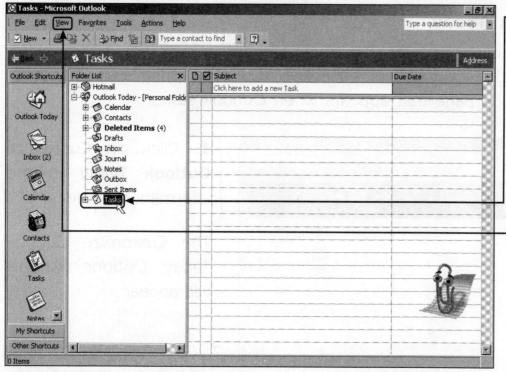

3. In the folder list, click on any folder that appears.

*The contents of the selected folder will appear in the **information viewer**.*

4. Click on **View**.

*The **View** menu will appear.*

5. Click on the **Folder List** in the View menu.

*The **folder list** will turn off.*

Outlook Today

Outlook Today is one of the icons on the Outlook bar. It displays a snapshot of all the items you need during the day.

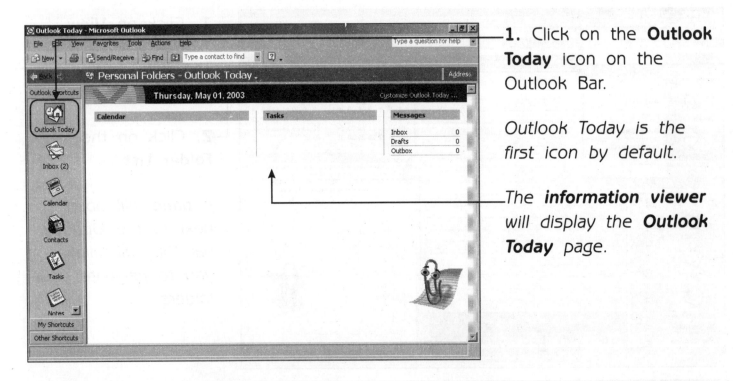

1. Click on the **Outlook Today** icon on the Outlook Bar.

Outlook Today is the first icon by default.

*The **information viewer** will display the **Outlook Today** page.*

Customizing Outlook Today

Outlook Today can be customized by you to display the folders you need, or to adjust the display of the calendar or task list. Outlook Today can be even programmed as the default page that appears when Outlook starts.

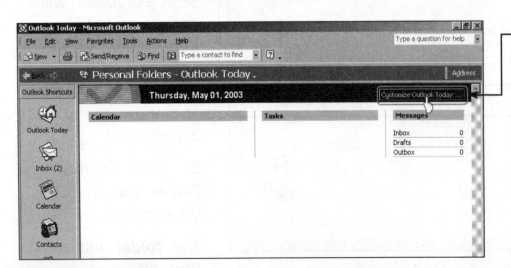

1. Click on **Customize Outlook Today** in the information viewer.

The Customize Outlook Today Options window will appear.

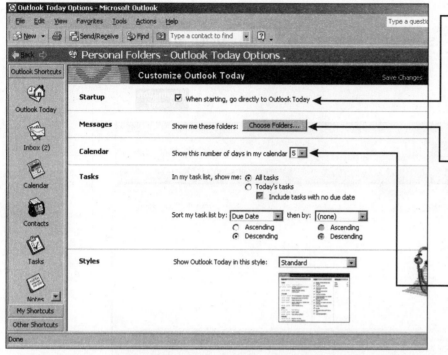

A. Startup: Click on the checkbox to make Outlook Today display your start page. Your start page will appear whenever you start up Outlook.

B. Messages: Click on the **Choose Folders** button to select which e-mail will appear on the Outlook Today page.

C. Calendar: Click on the drop down arrow to select the number of days to appear in the calendar.

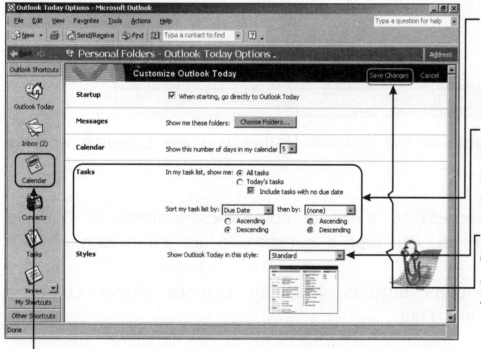

D. Tasks: Click on an option button to select a simple task list or today's tasks.

E. Styles: Click on the drop down arrow to select a layout style for the Outlook Today page.

2. Click on **Save Changes** at the top of the Customize Outlook Today screen.

Your new settings will be saved.

3. Click on the **Calender** on the Outlook Bar.

The Outlook Today window will close and the Calender will display in the information viewer.

Outlook Window

The Outlook window displays several items to help you in performing tasks efficiently.

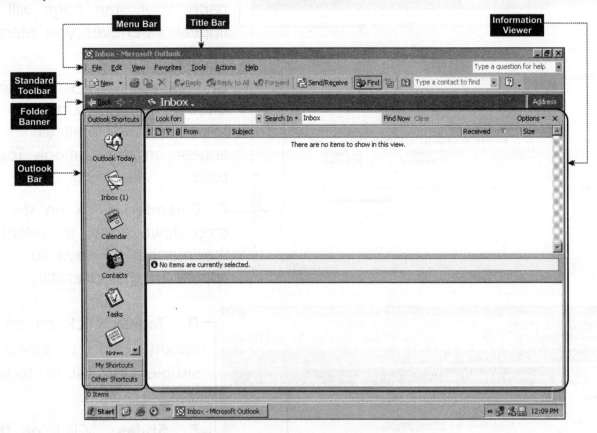

Title Bar: It shows the name of the Outlook feature you are currently working with.

Menu Bar: This provides access to a list of commands available in Outlook, and displays an area where you can type a question to get information.

Standard Toolbar: It contains buttons you can use to select common commands, such as Save and Print.

Folder Banner: This is the horizontal bar just below the Standard Toolbar. The Outlook navigation arrows, an icon for the active folder and the name of the active folder is displayed in the Folder banner. When the folder name is clicked, the Folder list shows the available folders and subfolders.

Outlook Bar: It provides access to the features included in Outlook. You can click the down arrow button on the Outlook bar to browse through the features.

Outlook Today

This allows you to view a summary for the current day.

Inbox

This allows you to compose e-mail messages and stores messages that you receive.

Calendar

This allows you to keep track of appointments.

Contacts

It contains an address book where you can store contact information.

Tasks

This allows you to create a list of things to do.

Notes

This allows you to create and store brief reminder notes.

Deleted Items

It stores items which you delete.

Information Viewer: It displays the Outlook feature you are currently working with.

2. Checking Mails

E-mail is the most important feature in Microsoft Outlook. Sending and receiving e-mail is now an integral part of doing business and communicating with others. You will need to know what to do with e-mail when you receive it.

Reading Messages

The e-mail messages you receive is stored in the **Inbox**. You can open a message to read the contents of the message.

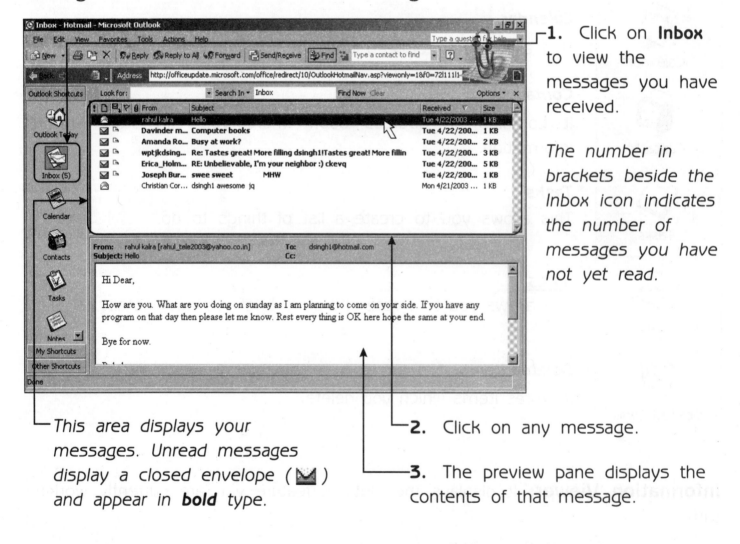

1. Click on **Inbox** to view the messages you have received.

The number in brackets beside the Inbox icon indicates the number of messages you have not yet read.

*This area displays your messages. Unread messages display a closed envelope ( ) and appear in **bold** type.*

2. Click on any message.

3. The preview pane displays the contents of that message.

Sending Message

You can send an e-mail message to express an idea or request information.

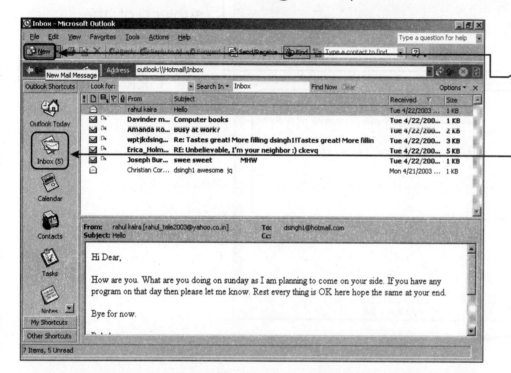

1. Click on **Inbox**.

2. Click on **New** to send a new message.

A window appears where you can compose the message.

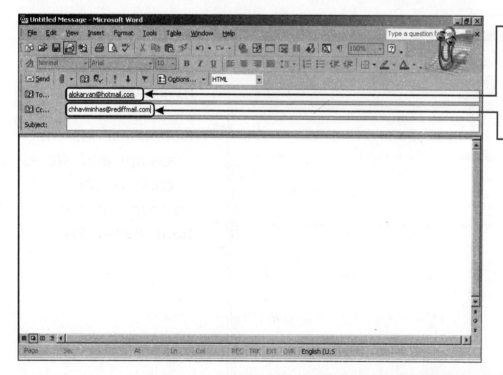

3. Type the e-mail address of the person you want to send the message to.

4. To send a copy of the message to a person who is not directly involved but would be interested in the message, click on this area and then type the e-mail address of the person.

To send a message or a copy of the message to more than one person in step 3 or 4, separate each e-mail address with a semicolon (;).

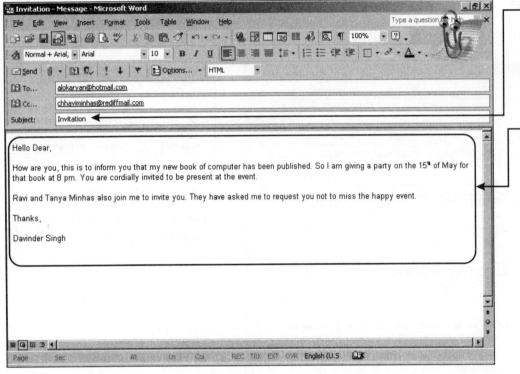

5. Click on this area and type the subject of the message.

6. Click on this area and type the message.

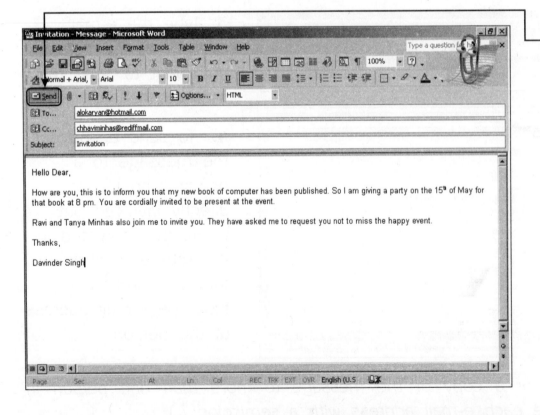

7. Click on **Send** to send the message.

*Outlook sends the message and stores a copy of the message in the **Sent Items** folder.*

Deleting a Message

A message that you no longer need can be deleted. Deleting messages prevent your folders from becoming cluttered with messages.

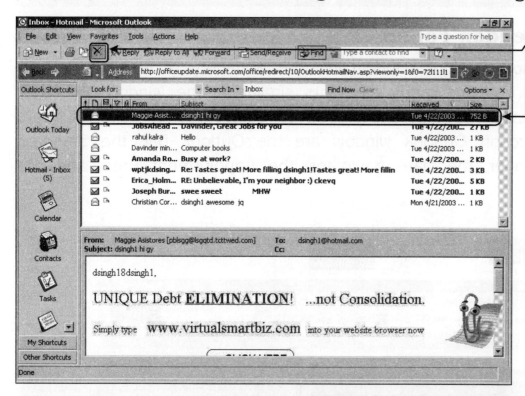

1. Click on the message you want to delete.

2. Click on the **Delete** button ( ) to delete the message.

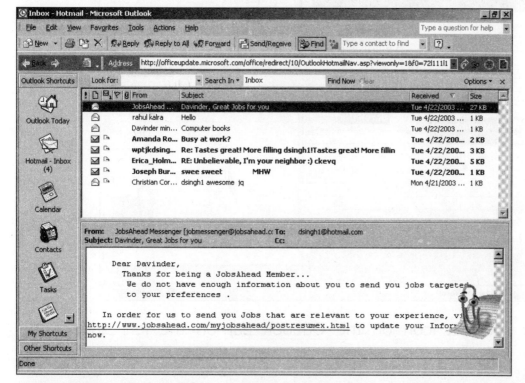

The message gets deleted.

Outlook places the message in the **Deleted Items** *folder.*

3. Calender

Opening the Calender Folder

The **Calendar - Microsoft Outlook** window includes a variety of features to help you work efficiently. It contains many elements similar to the windows in other applications, as well as some that are unique to Outlook. The main elements of the Calendar - Microsoft Outlook window are the Outlook Bar, the Standard Toolbar, the Folder Banner, the Date Navigator, the Appointment Area, and the TaskPad.

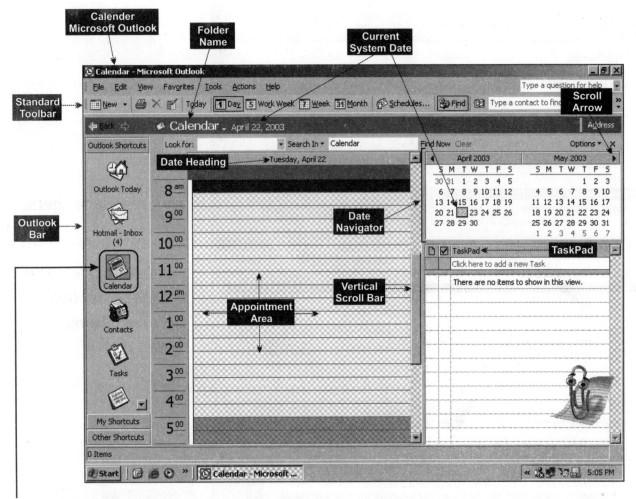

1. Click the **Calendar** shortcut icon on the Outlook bar on the left side of the screen.

Creating a Personal Sub-folder

You could enter appointments and events directly into the main Calendar folder, creating a daily, weekly, and monthly schedule, if you were the only person using Outlook on a computer. In many offices, several people share one computer and therefore need to create separate folders to store their appointments and events. With Outlook, you can create personal sub-folders to store your personal calendar and other files. Sub-folders then can be saved on the hard disk or a floppy disk.

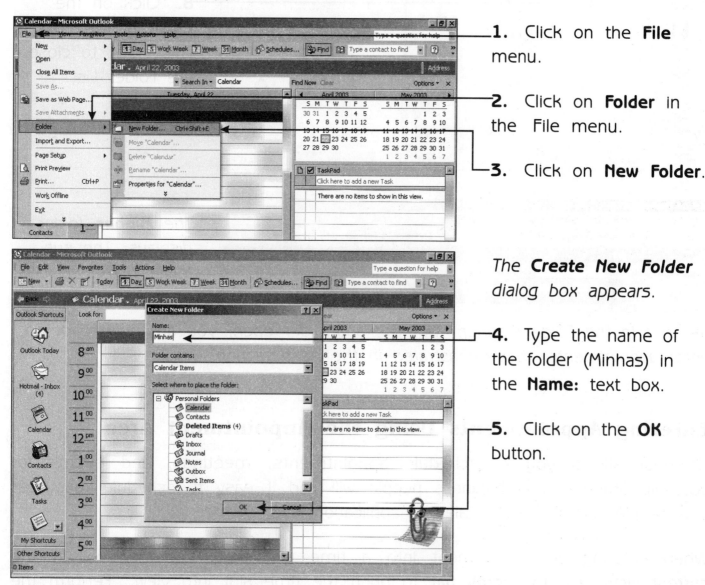

1. Click on the **File** menu.

2. Click on **Folder** in the File menu.

3. Click on **New Folder**.

The **Create New Folder** *dialog box appears.*

4. Type the name of the folder (Minhas) in the **Name:** text box.

5. Click on the **OK** button.

*The **Add shortcut to Outlook Bar?** dialog box will display.*

6. Click on the **No** button.

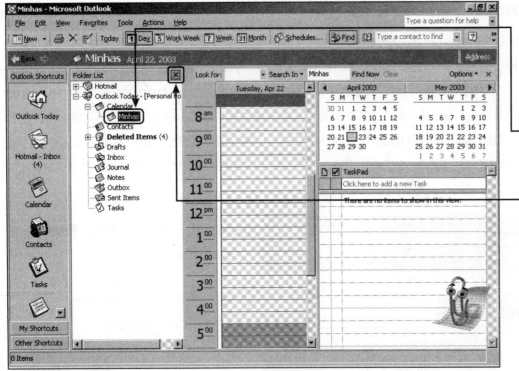

The **Folder List** appears in the left of the appointment area.

7. Click on the **Sub-folder** name.

8. Click on the **Close** button on the Folder List to close the Folder List.

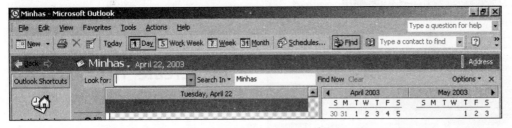

The **Minhas** folder displays. The sub-folder name displays on the Outlook Title bar and in the Folder banner. With the sub-folder open, you are now ready to enter appointments, as demonstrated in the next section.

Entering Appointments Using the Appointment Area

Calendar allows you to schedule appointments, meetings, and events for yourself. Students and business people will find it easy to schedule resources and people with Outlook's Calendar application.

When entering an appointment into a time slot that is not visible in the current view, use the **scroll bar** to bring the time slot into view. Perform the following steps to enter the appointments using the **appointment area**.

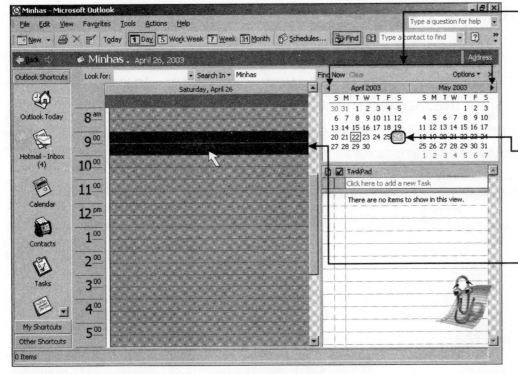

1. If necessary, click on the **scroll arrows** in the Date Navigator to display the month of your choice.

2. Click on the **date** in the Date Navigator to display it in the appointment area.

3. To make an appointment, drag through 9:00 am - 10:00 am time slot.

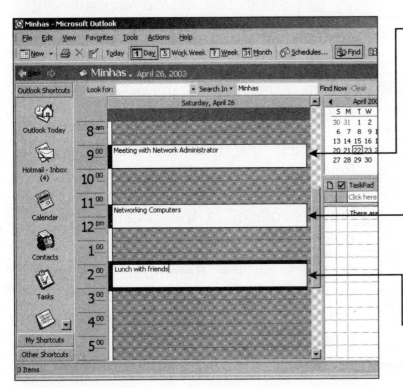

4. Type (Meeting with Network Administrator) in the dragged area as the first appointment.

As soon as you begin typing, the selected time slot changes to a text box with blue top and bottom borders.

5. Drag through the 11:30 am - 12:30 pm time slot. Type in (Networking Computers) the second appointment.

6. Drag through the 2:00 pm - 3:00 pm time slot. Type (Lunch with friends) the third appointment and then press the ENTER key on the keyboard.

The three appointments are displayed in the appointment area.

Entering Appointments Using the Appointment Window

You can enter appointments either by typing them directly into the appointment area, as shown in the previous section, or you can enter them using the **Appointment window.** Using the Appointment window is a slightly more involved process, but it allows specification of more details about the appointment.

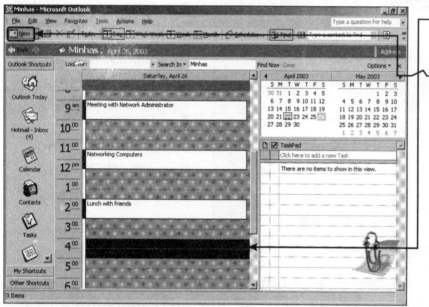

1. Drag through the 4:00 pm - 5:00 pm time slot.

2. Click on the **New Appointment** button on the Standard Toolbar.

The Untitled - Appointment window opens with the insertion point in the Subject text box in the appointment sheet.

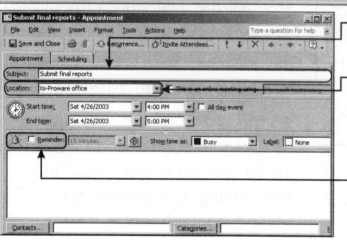

3. Type (Submit final reports) in the **Subject:** text box.

4. Press the **TAB** key on the keyboard to move the Insertion point to the **Location:** text box. Type (Xs-Proware office) in the Location text box.

5. Click on the **Reminder:** checkbox to instruct your computer to play a reminder sound before an appointment time.

A bell icon, called the Reminder symbol, displays next to appointments with reminders.

Both the subject and location of the appointment are displayed in the appropriate text boxes. Once typed, the appointment subject displays on the Appointment window Title bar and on the Taskbar button.

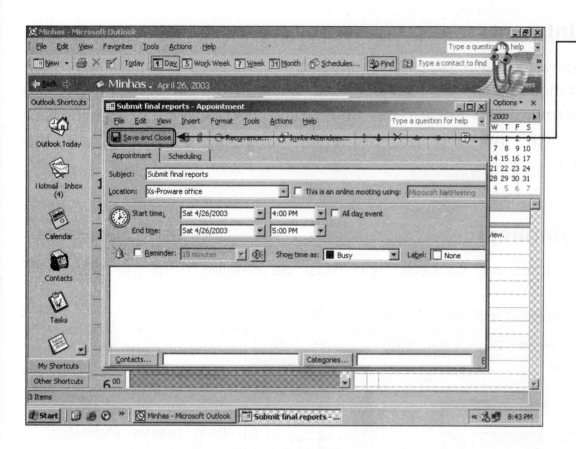

6. Click on the **Save and Close** button.

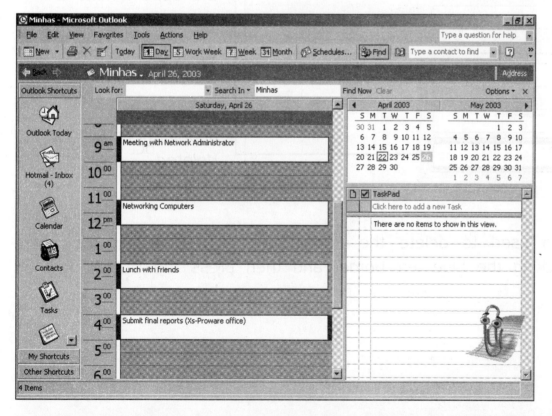

The schedule for Saturday, April 26 displays in the appointment area with the four new appointments entered.

Editing Appointments

Outlook provides several ways of editing appointments because schedules often need to be rearranged. Edit the subject and location of an appointment by clicking the appointment and editing the information directly in the appointment area, or double-click the appointment and make corrections using the Appointment window.

Deleting Appointment

Appointments sometimes are canceled and must be deleted from the schedule.

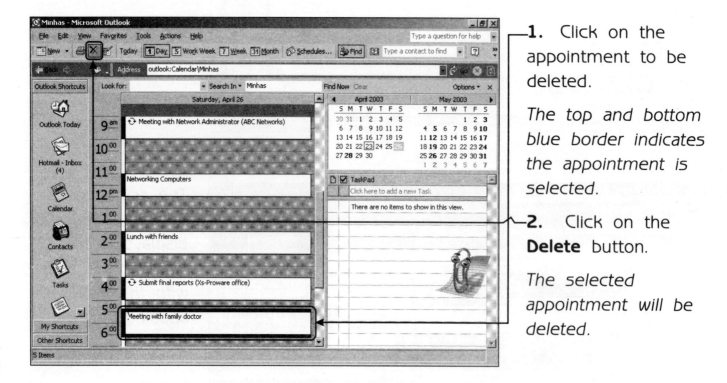

1. Click on the appointment to be deleted.

The top and bottom blue border indicates the appointment is selected.

2. Click on the **Delete** button.

The selected appointment will be deleted.

DELETE key is also used to delete the Appointments. First, select the entire appointment by clicking the blue left border and then press the DELETE key on the keyboard.

Moving Appointments to New Time

Outlook provides several ways to move appointments. Suppose for instance, that some friends cannot make it for coffee at 2:00 pm on Saturday, April 26, 2003. The appointment needs to be rescheduled to 1:00 pm. Instead of deleting and then retyping the appointment, simply drag it to the new time slot. The following steps describe how to move an appointment to a new time:

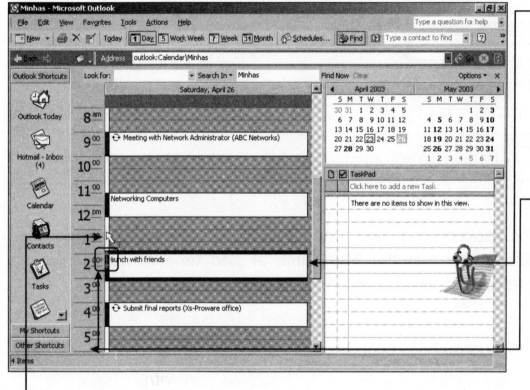

1. Click on the appointment which you want to move.

The blue border highlights the appointment.

2. Place the mouse pointer on the blue left border of the appointment.

The mouse pointer changes to a four-headed [✛] arrow.

3. Drag the appointment up to the time slot of your choice (1:00 pm - 2:00 pm).

As the appointment is dragged, the mouse pointer changes to a pointer with a small dotted box below it, called the drag icon.

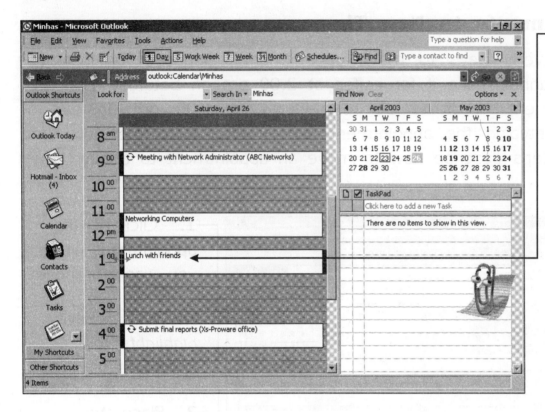

4. Release the mouse button to drop the appointment in the new time slot.

The appointment is placed in the 1:00 pm - 2:00 pm time slot. Outlook automatically allows adequate time for the moved appointment, in this case, one hour.

An appointment can be moved to a new time using the Appointment window, as well. Simply type a different time in the **Start time** or **End time** boxes or click on one of the time box arrows and select a different time in the list.

4. Using Tasks

Opening a Task

Now you can organize your daily appointments by creating an electronic to-do list of personal and work-related tasks that you want to accomplish.

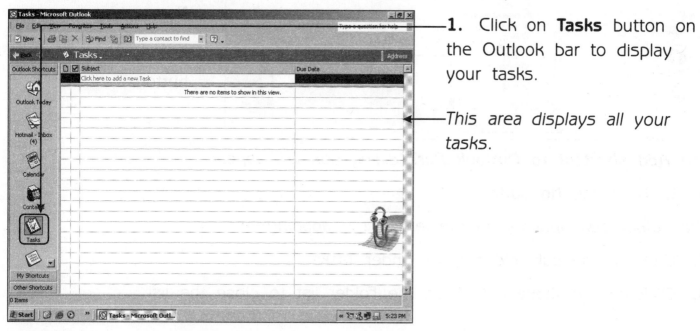

1. Click on **Tasks** button on the Outlook bar to display your tasks.

This area displays all your tasks.

Creating a Sub-folder

With Outlook, you can create personal sub-folders to store your personal tasks and other files. Sub-folders can then be saved on the hard disk or a floppy disk.

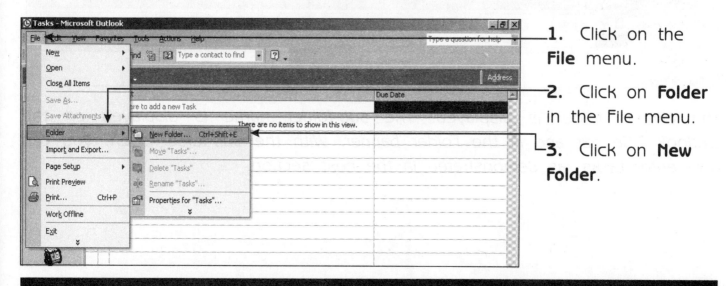

1. Click on the **File** menu.

2. Click on **Folder** in the File menu.

3. Click on **New Folder**.

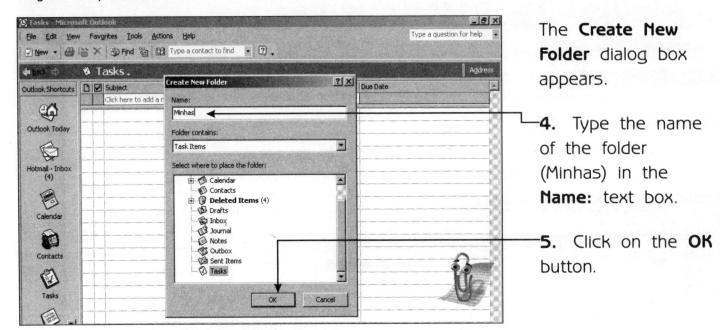

The **Create New Folder** dialog box appears.

4. Type the name of the folder (Minhas) in the **Name:** text box.

5. Click on the **OK** button.

The **Add shortcut to Outlook Bar?** *dialog box will appear.*

6. Click on the **No** button.

The **Folder List** *appears on the left of the appointment area.*

7. Click on the **sub-folder name** under Tasks.

8. Click on the **Close** button on the Folder list to close the list.

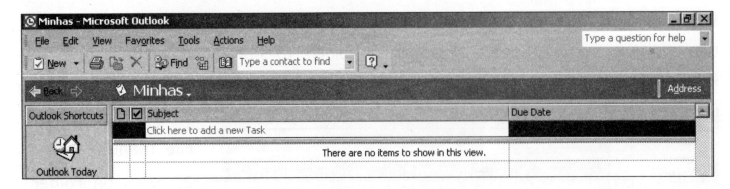

The Minhas folder is displayed. The sub-folder name is displayed on the Outlook Title bar and in the Folder banner. With the sub-folder open, you can now enter tasks, as demonstrated in the next section.

Creating a Task

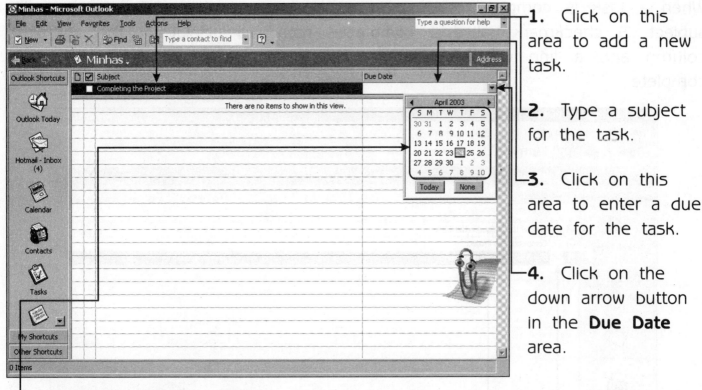

1. Click on this area to add a new task.

2. Type a subject for the task.

3. Click on this area to enter a due date for the task.

4. Click on the down arrow button in the **Due Date** area.

*The **Date Navigator** appears.*

5. You can click a date from the Date Navigator for due date.

*If your due date is the same day on which you are creating tasks, you can click on the **Today** button in the Date Navigator.*

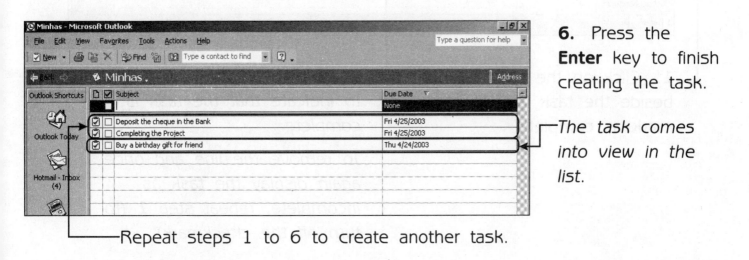

6. Press the **Enter** key to finish creating the task.

The task comes into view in the list.

Repeat steps 1 to 6 to create another task.

Marking a Task as Complete

When a task is complete, click on the checkbox on the left of the task's subject. A checkmark called a **completed icon** will display in the complete column and a line will be placed through the task indicating that it is complete.

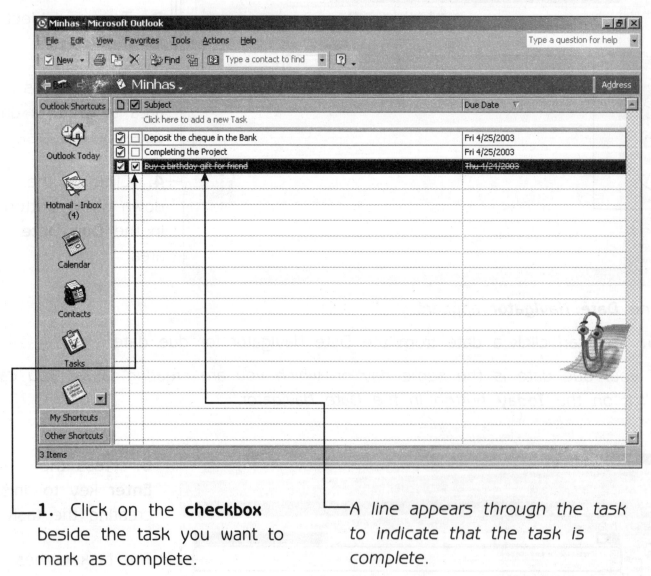

1. Click on the **checkbox** beside the task you want to mark as complete.

A line appears through the task to indicate that the task is complete.

To remove the line and once again display the task as incomplete, repeat step 1 (to turn off the checkmark).

Deleting a Task

To delete a task, select the task and then click on the **Delete** button on the Standard toolbar.

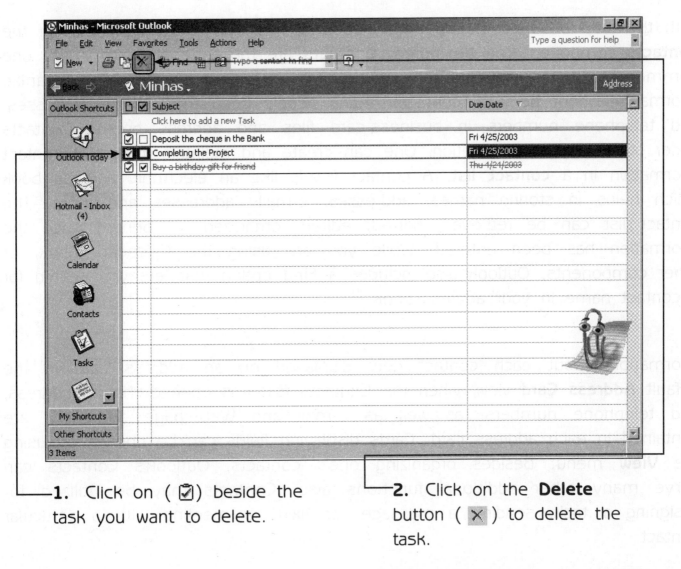

1. Click on (☑) beside the task you want to delete.

2. Click on the **Delete** button (✕) to delete the task.

The task disappears from the list.

*You can create tasks using **TaskPad** in the **Calendar** window to organize the many duties and projects for each day. The TaskPad, which displays below the **Date Navigator** in the Calendar window, allows creation of a **task list** of items that need to be tracked through completion.*

5. Contacts

With the help of Outlook, information about individuals or companies using the **Contacts** component can be stored. **Contacts** are those people with whom one communicates for educational, official or personal reasons. To organize information about personal contacts, many people keep the names, addresses, and telephone numbers in business-card files and address books. Contacts folder store contact information. One can create and maintain important contact information in a **contact list**. A contact list is like an electronic address book which helps in storing names, addresses, e-mail addresses and more. The contact list can be retrieved, sorted, edited, organized, or printed once the information has been entered. While you are using the Calendar, Inbox, or other components, Outlook also includes a **Find** option that lets you search for a contact name in your address book.

Information about each contact gets displayed on an address card in the default **Address Card** view, when the Contacts folder is opened. Name, address, and telephone numbers, as well as e-mail and Web page addresses are contained in each address card. Cards displaying fields can be chosen by using the **View** menu. Besides organizing one's contacts, Outlook's Contacts can serve many other additional functions also. Contacts may be utilized for assigning a task, sending a message, or fixing a meeting with a particular contact.

A contact list can also serve the purpose of an e-mail address book. Clicking on the contact's Web page address helps in accessing an Internet URL through Contacts. An addressed message box gets displayed ready for use if the contact's e-mail address is clicked.

Creating a Personal Subfolder in the Contacts Folder

The first step in creating the contact list is to create a personal subfolder. When only one person is working on a computer, a contact list can be stored in the Outlook's Contacts folder. If your computer is being shared, you will probably want to store your contact list in a personal subfolder.

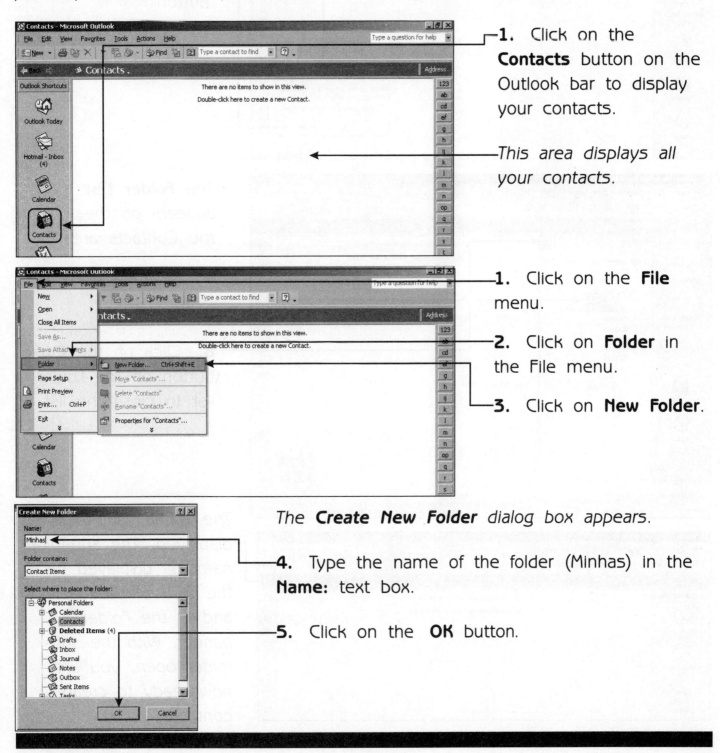

1. Click on the **Contacts** button on the Outlook bar to display your contacts.

This area displays all your contacts.

1. Click on the **File** menu.

2. Click on **Folder** in the File menu.

3. Click on **New Folder**.

*The **Create New Folder** dialog box appears.*

4. Type the name of the folder (Minhas) in the **Name:** text box.

5. Click on the **OK** button.

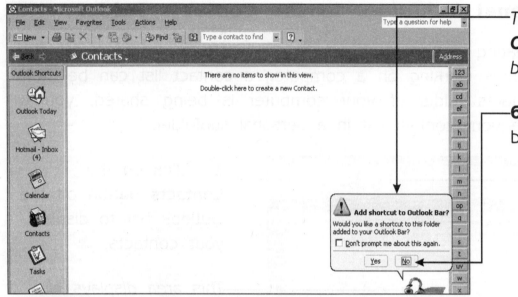

The **Add shortcut to Outlook Bar?** dialog box gets displayed.

6. Click on the **No** button.

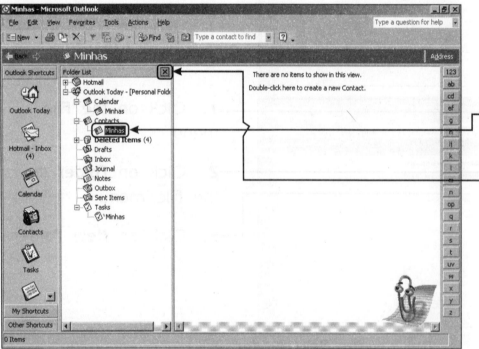

The **Folder List** appears on the left of the Contacts area.

7. Click on the sub-folder name.

8. Click on the **Close** button on the Folder list to close the list.

The Minhas sub-folder is displayed. The sub-folder name is displayed on the Outlook Title bar and in the Folder banner. With the sub-folder open, you are now ready to create contacts.

Creating Contacts

To make the contacts, follows these steps:

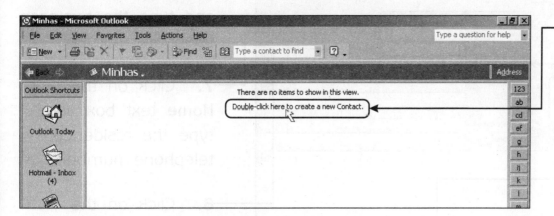

1. Double-click on **Double-click here to create a new Contact** in the contact area.

*The **Untitled – Contact** window will open. General contact information can be entered in this window.*

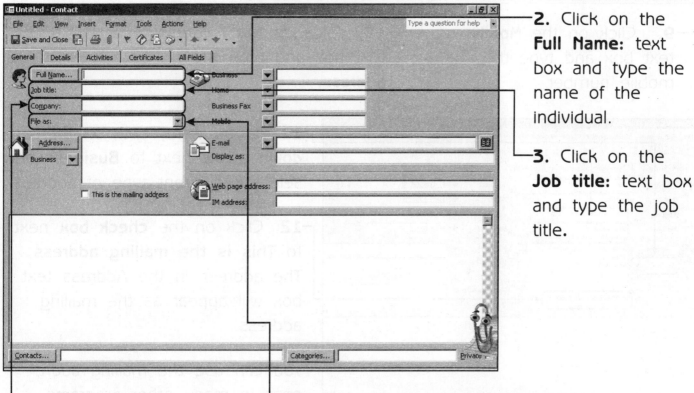

2. Click on the **Full Name:** text box and type the name of the individual.

3. Click on the **Job title:** text box and type the job title.

4. Click on the **Company:** text box and type the name of the company.

5. Click on the **down arrow** next to the **File as:** list box and select a filing scheme from the drop-down list.

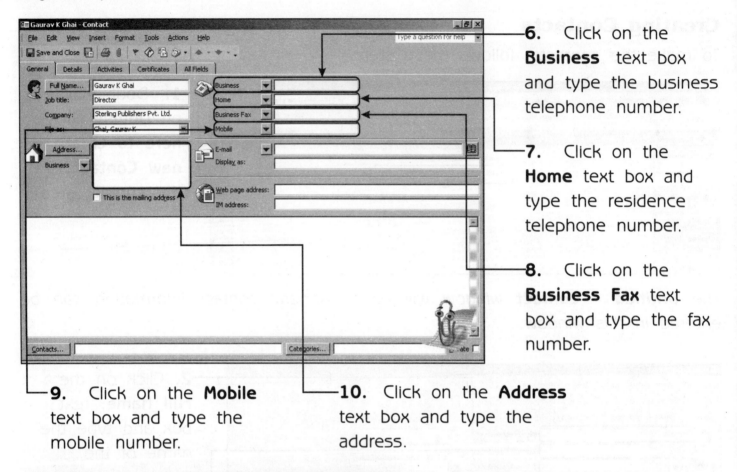

6. Click on the **Business** text box and type the business telephone number.

7. Click on the **Home** text box and type the residence telephone number.

8. Click on the **Business Fax** text box and type the fax number.

9. Click on the **Mobile** text box and type the mobile number.

10. Click on the **Address** text box and type the address.

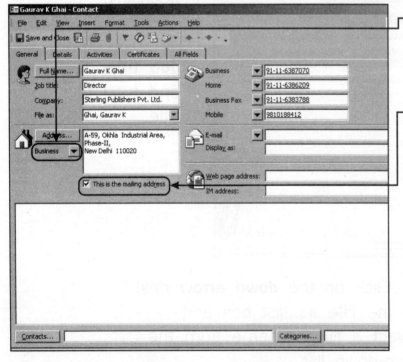

11. If you want, click on the **down arrow** next to **Business** and select a different type of address.

12. Click on the **check box** next to **This is the mailing address**. The address in the Address text box will appear as the mailing address.

You can use the mailing addresses in many other programs, like MS Word, when inserting an address from the contact list on an envelope or label.

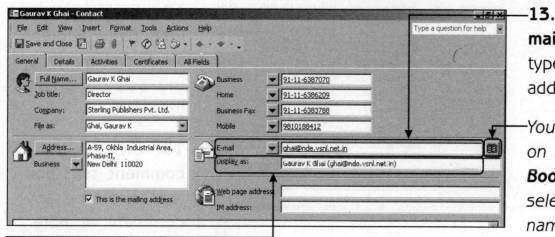

13. Click on the **E-mail** text box and type an e-mail address.

*You can also click on the **Address Book icon** and select an e-mail name from the list.*

Display as: *text box under the **E-mail** text box displays the name of the person and his e-mail address automatically.*

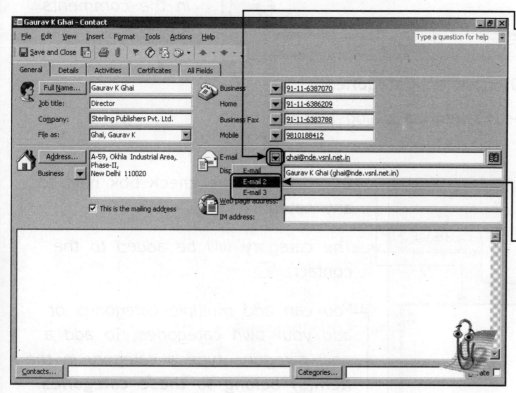

14. Click on the down arrow next to **E-mail** to add another e-mail address. You can store up to three e-mail addresses for each contact.

15. To store two or three e-mail addresses, click on **E-mail 2** or **E-mail 3**.

Your selection will appear in the list box and the insertion point will be in the text box.

16. Now type the additional e-mail address.

The address will appear in the text box.

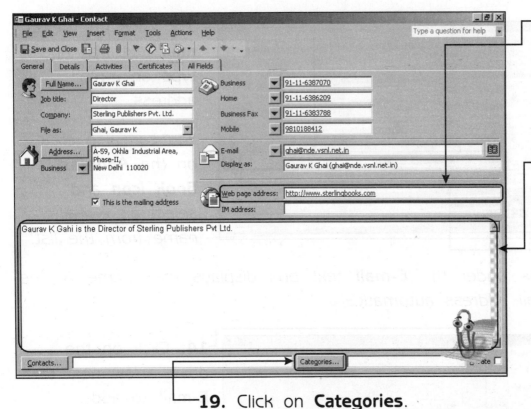

17. Click on the **Web page address:** text box and type the address of the Web site.

18. Click on the **comment** text box area and type any comment or note about the contact.

The text will appear in the comments area.

19. Click on **Categories**.

*The **Categories** dialog box will open.*

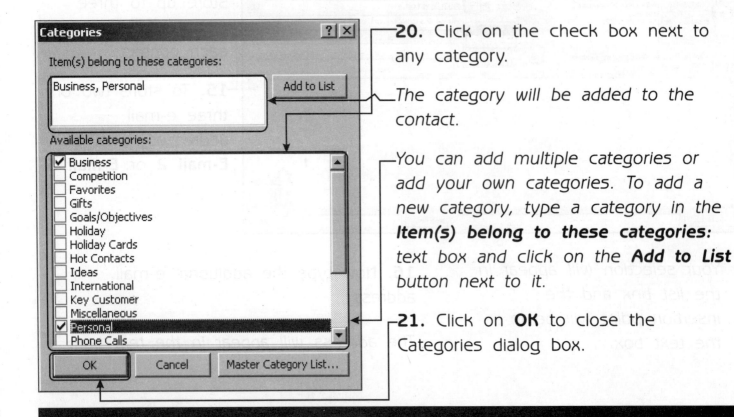

20. Click on the check box next to any category.

The category will be added to the contact.

*You can add multiple categories or add your own categories. To add a new category, type a category in the **Item(s) belong to these categories:** text box and click on the **Add to List** button next to it.*

21. Click on **OK** to close the Categories dialog box.

There are many more fields of information that can be added to the contact. Similar fields are organized together on the tabs of the Contact window.

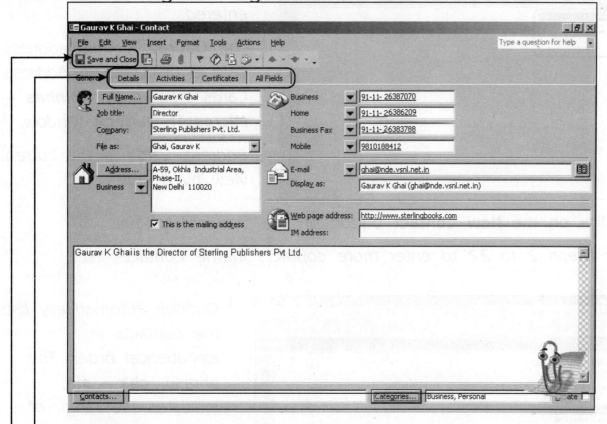

Details: Here you can enter information about the contact's birthday, anniversary, spouse's name, or department.

Activities: In this you can record details about letters, e-mails, or phone calls sent to the contact.

Certificates: If you have added additional security, here you can load security IDs in this tab.

All Fields: Here you can enter additional fields of information for the contact.

22. Click on **Save and Close**. *The contact will appear in the contact list.*

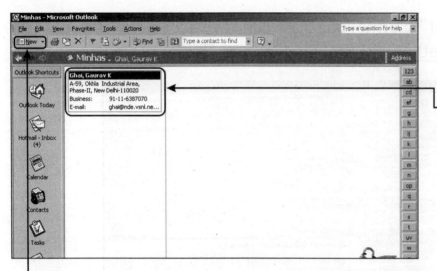

The Contact window displays the information you have entered.

*The **Gaurav K Ghai** address card is displayed in Address Cards view in the **Minhas - Microsoft Outlook** window.*

Address Cards is the current view by default.

23. Click on the **New Contact** button on the Standard toolbar.

Repeat Steps 2 to 22 to enter more contacts in the Contacts list.

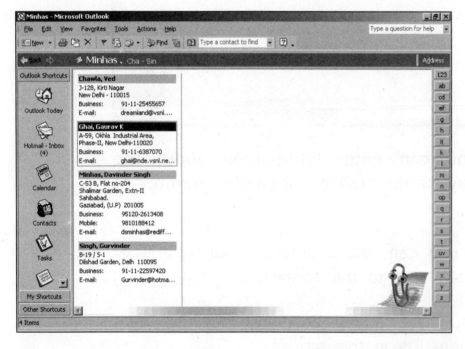

*Outlook automatically lists the contacts in alphabetical order. The phrase, **cha - sin**, indicates the range of contacts currently displayed (Chawla to Singh).*

Once the contact list is complete, it can be viewed, edited, or updated anytime. You can make some changes by typing inside the card itself. To display and edit all the information of a contact, double-click on the Address Card to display the Contacts window.